Coaching
MOTOR LEARNING, FITNESS and DEVELOPMENT
for
Young Children

Dr. Ramon Tejada

Kendall Hunt
publishing company

Kendall Hunt
publishing company

www.kendallhunt.com
Send all inquiries to:
4050 Westmark Drive
Dubuque, IA 52004-1840

Copyright © 2019 by Kendall Hunt Publishing Company

ISBN: 978-1-5249-8874-6

Published in the United States of America

TABLE OF CONTENTS

CHAPTER 3

BRAIN BENEFIT, BALANCE, EYE SIGHT, AND HEARING   19

- Brain Benefit And Exercise for Young
- The Need of Physical Education for Young Children
- The Importance of Balance
- Balance and Coordination
- Eyesight and Hearing

CHAPTER 4

SKELETOR AND MOOSECULES   29

- Muscular Development
- Muscle Control
- Height and Weight
- An Effective Physical Program for Young Children

CHAPTER 5

QUALITY MOVEMENT AND PHYSICAL EDUCATION   37

- Four Essential Components of Quality Physical Education
- Fundamental Movement Skills
- Types of Movement
- Understanding Biomechanics
- Key Principles of Biomechanics
- Principles of Biomechanic Inquiry
- Principle of Stability
- Biomechanics in Sport And Exercise
- Making Sense of Force
- Values in General, Linear, and Angular Motion

CHAPTER 6

NUTRITION AND HYDRATION   45

- Seven Signs of Insufficient Nutritional Value
- Nutrition and Living

- Make Meal Times A Life Priority
- Nutrition Education Activities for Children
- Hydration

CHAPTER 7

© Yaoinlove/Shutterstock.com

Photo submitted by Ramon Tejada

Ramon Tejada is a faculty member at California State University Channel Islands in Camarillo, California. His teaching areas are kinesiology; physiology of exercise; and motor learning, fitness, and development. He earned his degrees and completed his studies from California State University Northridge, Azusa Pacific University, and Walden University in the Doctoral of Philosophy program concentrating on Movement Education and its effect on skill and development in children. He has trained and worked at all levels of athletic development in the areas of basketball, football, soccer, track, and field. His expertise is in movement readiness and skill performance and proficiency. Dr. Tejada has written articles on increasing vertical leap jumping programs, depth drop resiliency, strength programs, and "the framework of the jump shot." Ramon continues in coaching and teaching movement education to students, student teachers, and coaches and how it serves young children in their development of motor skills and movement knowledge. *COACHING MOTOR LEARNING, FITNESS, AND DEVELOPMENT FOR YOUNG CHILDREN* helps to coach in the areas of motor movement skills with children who are attaining learning knowledge and connecting the skill experience for movement performance in a coaching delivery, focusing on age appropriateness for connectivity, process performance, and mastery.

> *"It is our professional duty to make sure we coach and work to develop young children, foundationally, with fundamentals, and addressing age appropriateness for developing their place in the world of movement, but it is our moral obligation to insure they receive the best movement coaching expertise can deliver."*

ACKNOWLEDGMENTS

To my family who continues to support the drive to achieve movement and passion.

The athletes and students who have given me an opportunity to learn, work, and excel in our aim to move proficiently and achieve.

To "Olin", a force that lives in all of us in reaching a "spirited merit."

INTRODUCTION

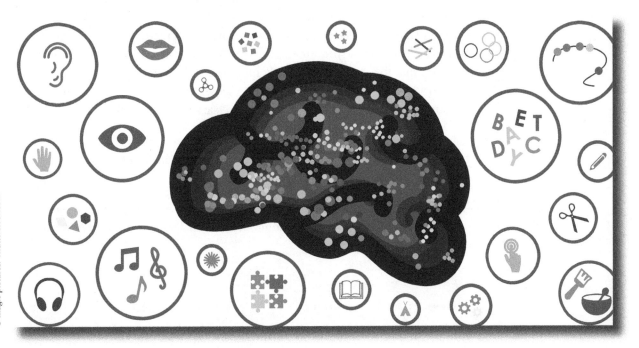

© magic pictures/Shutterstock.com

T his instructional manual of motor learning, fitness, and development explores comprehending child movement and skill attainment. It serves a purposeful understanding for those who observe and work to develop the learning process of movement skills for young children.

Motor development establishes a foundation for understanding its purposeful role on how it connects learning and movement for young children.

Motor development is the fundamental of the skeletal and muscle development in a child's capacity to demonstrate body and limb movement and to manipulate movement actions and skill attainment in the child's learning setting. Fine motor and gross motor are two areas of elemental processes that serve side by side for effective and focus on the recognition movement skills learned.

Movement activities and manipulation of objects are developmental fundamentals and a beginning exercise to connect learning for young children.

The recognition of skill attainment abides by expected progress in the motor development of the child. It is identifiable through the areas that are internal to body movement that rotates the head and neck, and the lifting of the arms and legs to reach movement recognition and manipulation. The external body movements like in the hands and feet, followed by finger and toe flexibility, are essential for a child's development of age progression continuing for other areas of the body.

Two areas that begin an understanding in connecting movement and learning are in the cognitive and social-emotional elements of development. The cognitive creates movement knowledge in the child's physical world, and the social-emotional will realize the child in activities such as talking, handling a cup to drink, and eating by picking up pieces of food while even using utensils.

The discipline in motor development is to stay on top of the child's day-to-day explorative, experiential, and developmental progressions. To observe, work, and coach young children in attaining motor skills is to guide and support the balance of the "mind and body," for achieving learning through movement. It is the recognition of moving and using those movements for children to express themselves and discover the things that they can do with body movement. Everyday life for young children should be a learning experience where they experiment and try different things that draw curiosity and imagination for using and learning motor skill execution.

Motor development assesses four targets that check for understanding in the area of developmental progression (the child developing at his or her growing pace) for movement skill attainment.

These four target areas are and will be foundational cornerstones that serve looked as the fundamental drivers for young children in learning and attaining motor development:

Physical Cornerstones

Cognitive Cornerstones   **Language Cornerstones**

Social and Emotional Cornerstones

© tomseven/Shutterstock.com

Chapter 1

ASPECTS OF MOTOR DEVELOPMENT IN YOUNG CHILDREN

When children are born, they are not able to move much on their own from their fetal setting. Motor development involves learning how to use muscles in sequence with body movement. The progression of acquiring motor skills begins basic and progresses to multifaceted.

Motor development happens in children at an unprecedented pace, but age in children can determine the differences in progression for skill development. We see when children begin to walk on their own at age level, yet some start to walk earlier, sit up, and manipulate objects at a noticeable degree.

The brain, which we will talk about more in depth later on, initiates a form of a command to movement by initial responses involuntary manner. It is true that children are born with reflexes that are intuitive to their nature for survival, but these necessary responses develop into a stronger will of learned and developed movement through maturation.

Muscular development and energy used by children are essential and good practice while young children are awake building coordination and strong arm and leg movement. The brain receives learning movement actions that it records in memory to facilitate future body movements that happen without thinking about doing them.

FUNDAMENTAL ASPECTS OF DEVELOPMENT

Motor development depends on the biology of children and their level of maturity. Our muscles, the skelctal, and the nerve structure are drivers for an efficient manner to execute a movement. This execution of movement follows developmental steps that coordinate with developmental age progression. Many times, it can be observed in some that children's actions can be inconsistent in their development where progress turns into regression and so forth. The observation process and coaching the development of motor skills keep this acquisition of learning motor skills visible.

THE VALUE OF CEPHALOCAUDAL

Children show development from the top to the bottom, meaning from their head to their toes. This element is known as *cephalocaudal (head-to-toe growth), physical and functional development*. During this phase of development, the head is more significant than most parts of the child's body. In thought, cephalocaudal looks at muscular development from the head down to the neck, to the superior portion of the body, to the arms, and, finally, down to the inferior part of the trunk, and the legs (gross motor). Motor development during the early years is about the head and neck skill and management movement. What follows is hand movements (fine motor) and the process of attaining the necessary alignment of eye–hand coordination. A developmental time during these phases work to ensure sequence in observable changes in the upper body, while the trunk, arms, and legs deliver motor learning skills for sitting, crawling, standing, walking, and a smooth run motion.

SENSE OF PROXIMAL DISTAL

It is attractive to motor development practitioners that the center of a child's body begins the process for motor skill attainment. This element is known as *proximal–distal*, sensing movement that begins center to out and close to now.

This sense of detection first sees the head and trunk progress movement of the arms and legs and then the fingers with the toes. Children experience a will to manipulate their arms and legs. The hands and feet follow this sequence of actions, leading to a discovery of their fingers and toes.

As children develop, we reflect on movements that come to alignment and proficiency involving all of the body to the use of particular body parts. To begin with, we see holding feeding objects with both hands practicing and gaining experience of moving toys and many other objects they learn to manipulate.

MOTOR DEVELOPMENT INSIGHTS

Motor highlights are the skills that involve each motor movement: skill attempted and observed by children in motor development. A point to remember that children learn at a different pace due to their developmental stage so a variance will occur with children. Motor highlights depend on genomic dynamics, taking into consideration of the parents and their motor learning attainment of skills.

We know and facilitate two practices in motor development: the area of high motor attainment and small finger and hand motor attainment. The two methods in motor development bring about a child moving from dependency to independence.

THE VALUE OF GROSS MOTOR DEVELOPMENT

© graphic-line/Shutterstock.com

Gross motor development looks for the skills that sequentially pull together the large muscle groups of a child's body. The arms, legs, and trunk are large and heavy muscle areas that work to develop sitting, walking, rolling around, standing erect, running, and kicking an object.

THE VALUE OF FINE MOTOR DEVELOPMENT

© Nataliya Turpitko/Shutterstock.com

Finger and hand motor development looks at skill attainment of the smaller muscles (such as hand, fingers, and face), including holding and picking up pieces of Cheerios, crayons, buttons, zippers, and turning pages of a picture or storybook.

In excellent motor skills, the small muscles of the hands and the eyes are observable movements and actions that young children demonstrate while practicing and experiencing visual contacts and stretching their body. Young children work to learn about their world with their eyes.

Young children learn to clench at a very early stage when one touches the palm of an infant, and its fingers will coil around to lock in and grasp. This coiling of the child's fingers is a reflex that will improve and develop into more skillful actions.

EVALUATION OF GROSS AND FINE MOTOR DEVELOPMENT

Assessment instruments can determine the performance of children in the area of gross and fine motor skills. Like all assessments, they need to provide good observational skills from the individual who is administering the assessment. Every assessment requires evaluating the child's developmental capability to demonstrate a motor skill. Professionals use the outcomes to determine the child's need in the areas tested for intervention if there is a need.

Experience and motor activity play is a vital role in children's motor learning. This awareness of movement discovery adds to the human makeup in motor development. In this field of understanding motor development, the ranks of practitioners see young children incorporating social knowledge to influence their motor behavior in physical movement difficulties, and it may provide an opportunity to be creative in movement knowledge and movement skills development that connects how the child learns.

A practitioner needs to be alert on the children who are not keeping up to par in gross motor, and (fine) finger and hand motor development is essential for keeping up on their progress and development.

When children do not demonstrate the motor skills at the proper levels, their motor development and skill attainment need consideration by a professional. The danger here is that we as practitioners want our children to progress on a level and regular sequential manner. When the motor skills of the child do not advance, a child may be in danger of falling behind on motor learning and social, experiential development.

© DGLimages/Shutterstock.com

SUMMARY OF PERCEPTUAL, GROSS, AND FINE MOTOR DEVELOPMENT

Perceptual Development

© Ozgur Coskun/Shutterstock.com

Perceptual skills attainment is happening all while the child is awake. Vision and hearing are occurring, the child takes eye pictures, seeing light shapes, sounds, familiar images, smells, and recording them. It is this practice and experience learning that improves and develops the perceptual movement of children adding to the social-emotional learning.

Gross Motor Development

© MNStudio/Shutterstock.com

Gross motor development attains skills such as rolling over, sitting up, crawling, walking, and running. Gross motor actions enable a child to move and pursue a variety of learning experiences and movements in their environment. They participate in developmental processes that enhance cognitive development, as they become great (copy-cats) imitators. When children are outdoors and demonstrating gross motor play with their counterparts (other children), it places them in the alignment of social skill development and learns to negotiate and use a rule to play.

Fine Motor Development

Small motor experience in young children gives way to observing finger and hand coiling, gripping, and manipulation experiential senses, people, and objects as children practice and learn in their environment.

Small hand muscle motor development leads to developing in areas of drawing, writing, and engaging in habits, such as feeding and getting cleaned up. An essential part of actions using fine motor movements of the hands is the coordination with perceptual information provided through movement of the eyes. Fine motor movements present a pathway of learning to proficient hand–eye skills.

© ChameleonsEye/Shutterstock.com

WORKSHEET FOR CHAPTER 1

Write a one-page reflection on aspects of motor development in young children.

_____

_____

_____

_____

_____

_____

_____

_____

_____

_____

_____

_____

_____

_____

_____

_____

_____

_____

_____

_____

_____

_____

Chapter 2
DOMAINS OF MOVEMENT

The domain of movement in children's development intertwines with children attaining movement skills and movement knowledge. Child development looks at growth and learning. There are four domains of child development, including:

- Physical – the development, growth, and maturation of a child's body, skeletal, muscles, and senses.
- Affective: Social – the child plays, speaks, and interacts movement tasking/Emotional – the child's self-awareness, about feelings, care, and interaction with himself or herself with others.
- Cognitive – children's thinking, how they reason, critically think, problem solve, and comprehend the use of language.
- Motor skills – movements and actions (fine and gross motor skills) that children develop skills in movement learning.

CHILD DEVELOPMENT AREAS

The domains influence each other in connecting different movement areas of representation and demonstration on the part of the child. Attainment of movement skills and movement knowledge in children develop early and are foundational for advancing movement skills and movement knowledge.

All children develop at his or her own pace of maturation. Therefore, parents and professionals who work and care for children need to be vigilant in the development of children.

We know children develop in a foreseeable direction, from an observable level to more multifaceted abilities. Children learn by exposure and run-through different movement skills and thought through play. Play becomes an essential prospect for children to exercise new skills.

We know there are many issues influencing child development in the sectors of their deoxyribonucleic acid (DNA), background experience and knowledge, heredity, family, and community. The early learning experiences in young children do affect their learning, development, and maturation timelines for life.

We need to make children's development at different ages and stages a purer form of understanding for parents and care professionals by:

- knowing expectations of children
- being aware and observant
- developing the third *eye* on the ages and stages of development
- being supportive and understanding

CHILDREN'S DEVELOPMENT AREAS

The developmental areas of children's growth are codependent in each level of growth. The development process prompts an increase in movement in other levels of maturation in young children.

Children in developmental pace need monitoring and observation in each area of developmental age and stage indicators. Development travels through and with child progression from birth through adolescence as they progress from complete reliance to self-sufficiency toward maturity. The relationship between maturation and learning contributes to the transformations of childhood growth.

PHYSICAL DEVELOPMENT

The area of real developmental talks about the development of a child's physical skills is recognized as motor skills. Motor skills are the movement attainment that provides children with actions, while acquiring the physical traits of their setting and themselves. It is this area of development children attain gross and fine motor management skills, equilibrium, and coordination of the eye to hand and hand to eye for movement awareness.

A growth chart and developmental scale that measures children by weight, height, and body scope for fitness are used to guide growth. Essential nutrition is paramount in keeping a child sound and illness free.

THE PART SENSES PLAY IN CHILDREN

Perception is an outcome of complex tasks that come out of brain development. The essentials that perception creates are needed to deliver the management and control of motor skills. When children acquire recognition, interpretation, learning, understanding, and reacting to a particular movement, they show maturation in the areas of social-emotional and cognitive ability. This learning experience gives way to attempts to practice, building awareness, and strengthening their movement skills in fine and gross development.

COGNITIVE DEVELOPMENT

Cognitive development is about, "the knowing," intellectual development and, "the expression," the creativity expansion. Intellectual development in children demonstrates:

- Managing thoughts
- Hold adequate attention
- Recalling the occurrences
- Environment interpretation
- Showing organization skills

When children interact with their environment, play, and connect with their peers, a child can create and imagine a world of expression that creates learning for their self and the mates they share their world.

Children's imagination and creativity is not limited to the use of materials. It is seen in their games when they use fantasy to mold their identity and create excellent opportunities for self-expression in different situations. Creativity generates the cognitive intelligence, occurrences practiced, and the everyday language that spells out the meaning of dreams.

LANGUAGE DEVELOPMENT

Language development comes to see language as a form of communication and comprehension in childhood development. As children learn and use speaking as a connection to things, peers, and authority, their verbal ability depends on how they will see and feel about themselves. Expressing words and sound delivery gives way to a communication skill for children that enhances their well-being, self-esteem, and identity. The correct use of words gives them what they want and will effectively build confidence. The thought process in young children manages to secure critical thinking and conversational pieces that enable exchanges in gestures, tone, and body language.

SOCIAL AND EMOTIONAL DEVELOPMENT

The area of social-emotional development looks at the ability children have in understanding expressions, emotions, play, and comprehending peer pressures. Children learn about feelings and how they make sense to them. They learn how to show or control emotions while talking about them and sharing them. Social behavior teaches children to cooperate, consider others, and be genuine in sharing with others. The social-emotional connection is essential to children's success in schools, relationships, and parenting.

SELF-ESTEEM DEVELOPMENT

This area where children feel unique about themselves approach things that challenge them with a critical thinking eye and feeling. A positive self-concept is a healthy self-esteem, feeling this way gives way to school success, making friends, and exercising team concepts for group participation. Instilling a self-concept will create respect for themselves, their family connecting the identity that represents their own. Now comes the way they look, they feel, a social persona, behavior, and their associations with others. Social status can influence the self-concept, leading the self-esteem and the mind–body–soul image that forms in young children.

Self-esteem can impact development in personality if issues come into play during activities. If children lack the self-concept/self-esteem, the social-emotional drive that touches school success may prevent them from feeling right about the things they do and how they see themselves feeling good about who they are. Personality is a creative and expressive aspect of young children; we as practitioners need to support them.

BUILDING GROUPS

In this group children develop leadership skills, cooperation, and consideration for others while connecting to peers and working relationships. Also, the focus becomes evident in differences, same sex, age, and ethnicity.

Moral development becomes real in children as they:

- Build morals and beliefs
- Develop a conscience

- Follow society's laws and regulations, and policies
- Build relationships and trust
- Learn to justify and reason
- Work to be fair and play fair

EMOTIONAL DEVELOPMENT

- Being as good as everyone else
- Understanding the self to feel part of the peer environment
- Accepting challenges and understanding let downs
- Being sensitive to others, empathy and judging feelings

SELF DEVELOPMENT

- Responsibilities
- Conversation and language

COGNITIVE SELF-REGULATION

- Movement knowledge-Movement skills

EMOTIONAL SELF-REGULATION

- Social-emotional and physical situations

© Suzanne Tucker/Shutterstock.com

© zdshutterman/Shutterstock.com

Chapter 3
BRAIN BENEFIT, BALANCE, EYE SIGHT, AND HEARING

Intellectual development begins with understanding the knowing in young children as they play to experience an experimentation learning into knowing.

Cognitive acquisition in children set the tone as they attain skills in using language, terms and vocabulary, and computation skills. Language happens early in children, and learning continues to develop in these areas to prepare a child in school readiness and for school success.

The areas of need in children for fundamental support in their physical development are:

- Nutrition and healthy planned foods
- Movement in physical activities, organized sports, and free play
- Exercise activities
- A learning environment where care, creativity, and expression are supported
- Being self-aware, conscious, and social-emotional well-being
- Critical thinking for problem-solving
- Focus and observant skills for attention and comprehension

Children, as they meet their intellectual development, show the capabilities of their brain benefit. In this learning environment, children begin to think, express ideas, and demonstrate organizational deliveries. Children start to connect with their world and the setting of experience.

As years progress in a child's life, the time is crucial looking at the beginning 5 years of their developmental years. This time is a commencing occurrence of a child becoming a person with personality traits that will embody them through their life span. During this time, learning how to conduct themselves, understanding what they can or not do, and experiencing motion come about in social skill development. The five characteristics of children stem from the different areas of development that human development serves as a guide to shaping and assessing ages and stages. These first 5 years are vital in the shaping of a child's social-emotional, mental-cognitive, and motor-physical development.

Brain benefit acquires social-emotional and motor-physical attainment in young children and other areas of development pursuing the young child to adult that they will form.

The following are the best practices to support brain benefit and development in young children:

1. Maintain a safe and caring environment
2. Support the learning climate and environment
3. Observe the areas and situations of exploration
4. Seek out networks for community and programs
5. Make sure child programs are the best quality and use best practices
6. Know how to get help
7. Speak, read, and listen
8. Good food and source of nutrients for brain benefit:
   • Eggs and salmon
   • Whole grains/oats/oatmeal
   • Blueberries, beans, colorful veggies, greens
   • Fruit is good for the brain
   • Avocados

Brain growth (intellectual) includes:

• Thought process
• Awareness
• Judgment
• Managing information

Children need various opportunities to plotting and making choices and be able to visualize results. Children using language, problem-solving, ask questions to assess and develop concepts and notions. Intellectual preparedness brings about singing, stories, and rhymes for word development. Here a child begins to name and describe pictures, colors, figures, and places. The imaginary mindset starts to contribute to aligning exploratory and experiential learning with language and speaking to a child's life inventory ideas and knowledge.

BRAIN BENEFIT AND EXERCISE FOR YOUNG

Children who participate in children games, structured and unstructured activities, develop endurance and fitness for their young and developing bodies. Children grow into sports, participate in vigorous physical activity, and play for enhancing their cognitive awareness and intellectual play organization. Exercise has many healthful benefits for children in the developing years. It gives the child balance and mental stability freethinking and expression while keeping the body moving and delivering movement in participating physical activities and games.

© Lorelyn Medina/Shutterstock.com

The following are practices to help keep children working to develop play participation and mental awareness in physical activities and exercise:

- A movement that involves training advances the blood flow to the brain
- Exercise builds new brain cells in brain sectors
- Practice makes the body's level of brain-derived neurons that leads to children's learning and knowledge
- Activity affects the shape and purpose of the children's brain. Fit children score better in cognitive challenges a vital part of the brain that supports maintaining attention and management control or the ability to coordinate actions and thoughts crisply
- Fit children experience complex thought, brain works for organization and purpose
- Exercise supports a child's ability to learn
- Practice assists creativity
- Exercise reduces stress, contributes to stabilizing body's chemistry, nervous system, and vital organ systems
- Children acquire relationships from fitness results to academic success
- Children who participate in attain confidence, teamwork, and leadership skill in organized sports and activities
- Exercise builds up a child's strength, flexibility, and endurance—the three crucial elements in fitness

The following are the steps on how to advance and motivate young children in movement activities:

1. Model to children by being active yourself
2. Fitness should be fun
3. Go on walks and hikes
4. Have fun running and rolling
5. Ride a bike
6. Move and dance, rhythmic movement
7. Teach competition responsibility
8. Be outdoor ready and outdoor participant
9. Make an active life fun living
10. Make sound judgments of children who play contact sports

THE NEED OF PHYSICAL EDUCATION FOR YOUNG CHILDREN

We as practitioners of physical education drive the notion of physical activities in young children to improve their muscle development, strength, flexibility, acknowledge fitness, body composition, and cardiovascular endurance.

The attainment of skill development of motor skills allows safe and secure, productive, and satisfying engagement in physical activities and exercise. This motive of support of movement education builds a lifelong stream for lifelong fitness.

The benefits of exercise in young children improve and show positive cognitive function working to attain motor skill development. Children who are active in physical activities do well in assessments and achieve academically. Being regular exercise participants adds to the brain's improvement of memory and thinking skills. Instilling the fitness and education part of exercise hopefully would have children learning to watch weight, lower blood pressure, prevent depression, and feel good to look better.

The role that exercise aids in young children is to advance their gross motor skills, such as running, kicking, throwing, and swinging. Regular physical activity can decrease children's risk of becoming obese and developing associated health problems, as well as promoting better sleep, while nutrition is playing a support role.

Physical activity helps children with coping with stress and anxiety. It encourages:

- Healthy growth and human development
- Self-esteem and self-identity
- Healthy bones, muscles, and joints.
- Statue, weight, posture, and balance
- A strong and healthy heart
- Weight control and skeletal support
- Social-emotional

The movement for the best brain benefit is aerobic exercise, such as running, swimming, and hopping. This exercise helps pump more blood to the brain and deliver more oxygen, making the blood flow up and down to the mind. However, if you do not move or exercise the body, it can incur body fat percentage, endurance levels, and insulin sensitivity. Moderate participation of movement activities and training can get your body moving, as in young children the brain and body movement activities can serve to defy health and disease.

THE IMPORTANCE OF BALANCE

© Ollyy/Shutterstock.com

Balance is the state of different energies that come together and present a level of stabilizing these energies. Equilibrium is the form where uneven effects bring together and balance one another. Balance is a central skill needed to maintain and manage positions, such as sitting in a chair, participating in physical movement and activities, running, and riding a bike. A child learning about balance makes motor skill development more comprehensible while learning to use both the mind and the body to try skills and be successful in school.

Working on balance skills for youth is foundational and fundamental training needed for managing controlled skills, such as sitting in a chair or engaging in physical activities like running or riding a bike. Having balance makes movement development easier, reduces safety concerns, and helps children focus on academic assignments.

BALANCE AND COORDINATION

In movement skills, we talk about looking at balance and coordination for children being healthy and safe. Balance works to maintain a skillful body position while performing a skill. Children learn to function effectively in and out of environments and movement skills, the ability needed to support skilled positions during both stationary and active activities. Stable balance is the skill to hold a quiet spot with control, freeze tag, green light–red light stopping games. Dynamic stability is the skill to remain balanced while performing a movement, such as riding a bike and skating. The importance of balance and coordination working together looks at age-appropriate movement and skill activities that involve both balance and co-ordination. Here the child experiences sports participation with an experiential level of success as it supports flexible body movement for physical skill performance. Involvement in sports aids in maintaining self-regulation for everyday skill performance while working in social-peer networking and attaining a feeling of fitting in a community or social environment.

EYESIGHT AND HEARING

In general, children experiencing balance disorders show symptoms of disequilibrium, meaning wavering, "dizzy" feeling that causes difficulty in standing up, walking, turning around and around with slow dizzy recovery, bump corners, or ascent the stairs with feelings of unskillfulness. Balance disorders can affect vision problems as seeing plays a stabilizer role in maintaining the same movement.

Hearing does not cause balance disorders, but difficulties with the inner ear that are accountable for sounds and the vestibular system may make the equality of movement stabilizing difficult. Besides, hearing loss happens jointly with balance loss symptoms and can show a causal condition related to keeping balance if fluid has impaired the ear or sinus area.

To develop balance and coordination, children need a foundation and fundamental in achieving an instructive approach to maintaining and controlling skill equilibrium. The following are instructional tips for balance and coordination:

- Focus and attention
- Awareness and savvy
- Two-sided integration
- Boundary midline
- Hand–eye skills
- Hand control
- Muscular strength
- Muscular endurance
- Self-regulation
- Posture control
- Body awareness
- Sensory processing
- Isolated movement

Children who are challenged with balance and coordination might be identified here:

- Fall easily
- Lack fluid body movement
- Avoid physical participation
- Late to reach developmental indicators
- Slower than their peers in physical skills
- Peers more skillful in refined sports participation
- Invade the personal space of peers more than they mean to
- Fearful of new physical games
- Difficulty assisting oneself getting dressed standing up
- Trouble navigating some settings
- Tire more quickly than their peers
- Motor skill planning
- Flabby or tense muscle tone
- Spatial awareness
- Low endurance of physical tasks
- Writing skill development
- Pencil grip
- Pencil management
- Left-right discrimination
- Hand dominance
- Articulation
- Sensory processing

It's been the experience of coaches and teachers in the area of balance and shaping coordination in motor skills in young children needing screening and pre-assessments. Establishing a benchmark to focus on a starting point benefits the progression and advancement of achieving success in movement activities.

© GraphicsRF/Shutterstock.com

Chapter 4
SKELETOR AND MOOSECULES

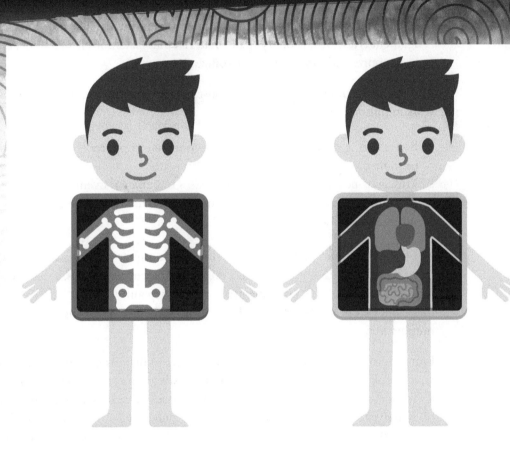

The bone and skeletal structure of the human body is a durable frame that lends the structure for a purpose. The skeleton contracts and expresses reduction of muscle movement attaching to tendons that serve as connectors.

Various animals possess skeletons to aid and defend their physical frame to assist in its movement. When talking of the human skeleton, the bone structure comprises bone growth and expansion. The skull shields the brain, and the ribs shield the heart and the lungs. Nevertheless, what we need to know precisely is how our bone structure and skeletal frame support our weight for a smooth flow of the body.

At birth, an infant's body contains 300 bones. These bones will merge to establish growth to 206 bones that form and show presence once reaching adulthood. Some of the baby's bones are made entirely of a material known as *cartilage*. This bone structure during the early growing years works together to mend and align themselves with finishing the final formation of the skeletal system.

Getting to know the muscle system lends itself to understand their function. The muscles work to tug on the joints, creating movement activity. Tendons connect to the bone, for example, in the legs and our arms. This type of pull-and-push movement occurs in our body. For example, in the tendons binding muscles and to structural body entities, such as in the legs, our arms, and the face. The function of the tendon is to move the bones and other structures like movement flight. A ligament is a sturdy, rubbery tissue material that fastens itself to a bone, and the bone supports body structures to stabilize them.

Movement occurs when the bones, muscles, tendons, and ligaments combine to work in unison.

1. Bones are a durable tissue-type material that supports our weight without bending.
2. Muscle tissue causes contraction and eases to initiate movement.
3. Tendons are tissue material that connects the muscles to a bone from a strong, sturdy, but flexible material.

In bone development and frame structure, the number of bones may sometimes differ in individuals, but in normal developmental circumstances, at best, humans have 206. Research and site information may explain variation in bone development, but for our fundamental understanding and usage, we acknowledge the bone number 206.

Our skeletal structure for our usage in working to help us develop motor skill has now established a little understanding of knowing the bone growth in young children. Now, we move on to the muscles in our body. The muscles exercise action to body parts by contracting and relaxing. They employ jointing flexors and extensors, kind of rubber band types. There are other types of muscles, such as your cardiac muscles, which involuntary muscles movement in both cases.

When muscles labor by expanding and contracting parts of the body, a muscle contains long, skinny cells that form a cluster into groups. A muscle thread receives a sign from its adjacent nerve; proteins and then chemicals deliver a shot of energy to make the muscle contract for working form or for reducing its force, making the muscle contract draws the bones to a connected state bringing them close together.

A good explanation of bones that support the human body and assist in forming our framework is as follows. Bones can be light but are strong enough to sustain the weight that our skeletal frame exists for maximum health.

Let us understand that bones also serve as a guard to the human skeleton and protect the organs in our body. The skull guards the brain and shapes the face. The spinal cord sends points of information between the mind and the body, which are guarded by the spinal column. The ribs are a cage-like housing guarding the heart and lungs, and the pelvis protects the bladder, part of the intestines, and, in females, the reproductive organs.

Bones consist of a protein known as *collagen*, which is made up of a mineral called calcium phosphate that strengthens the framework for toughness and stability. Bones supply calcium which is delivered into the bloodstream. The amounts of some vitamins and minerals that we consume, mainly vitamin D and calcium, dictate how calcium is stored in the bones. The bones are two tissue types: compact bone and cancellous bone. A bone is a hard and solid material that carries blood vessels and nerves that channel through the holes that they possess. Cancellous bones move the bone marrow found in the compact bone. The bone marrow comprises stem cells, red blood cells, platelets, and white blood cells. Red blood cells transport oxygen to the tissues of the body, platelets aid blood clotting, and white blood cells take on infections when a cut of the skin occurs. One of the critical components in bone stability that attached bone to other bone is elongated, fibrous straps called *ligaments*. Cartilage is a bendable, rubbery material in the joints that helps and guards bones where they brush against each other.

The bones in children are smaller than those in adults and have areas of growth known as *plates*. These plates consist of many cartilage cells growing long, and transforming into hard, mineralized type bone. As bones develop through life, the body frame continuously renovates and reshapes bone living tissue. Bone includes three types of cells: osteoblasts (make new bone and repairs damages), osteocytes (mature bone cells continue development in a new birth frame), and osteoclasts (break down bone and sculpt and shape its forms).

Understanding muscle development and their functions is essential to a precise movement for bone and collaboration. Muscles tug on the joints, causing change. Muscles help the heart in its rhythmic motion, the chest lifts and descends when breathing, and blood vessels control blood's pressure and flow. The three types of muscles found in the human body are skeletal muscle, involuntary muscle, and cardiac muscle; skeletal muscle is attached by tendons to bone, such as in the legs, arms, and face. These muscles support the skeleton, give the body form, and assist with everyday movements. Involuntary muscle is made of fibers and has a smooth and silky appearance. We cannot willfully control our smooth muscle; the nervous system automatically manages and controls without thought. Smooth muscles take a bit of time to contract compared to skeletal muscles, if they do not fatigue. Cardiac muscle is heart muscle. The walls of the heart's cavities are completely made of muscle fibers. Cardiac muscle material is an involuntary type of muscle. Its rhythmic, strong contractions move blood out of the heart as it beats sending blood to all necessary inlets and outlets.

MUSCULAR DEVELOPMENT

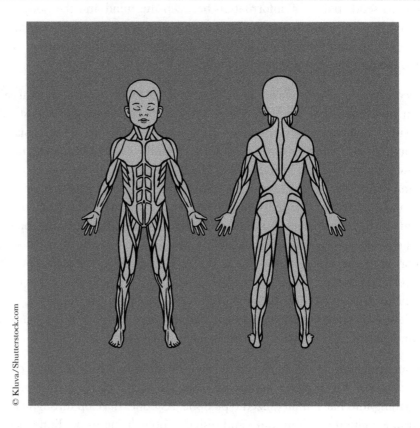

© Kluva/Shutterstock.com

Essential aspects of muscles support development in young children to keep balance and to master motor skills and movement knowledge. The following are questions to render:

• How tall will I be?
• How much weight will I carry?
• Can I develop gross motor skills, strong legs, and purposeful muscle work?
• Can I develop fine motor skills—manipulation of my muscles in my hands?
• Will I learn to be balanced and be coordinated?
• Can I be strong and build muscle strength?

MUSCLE CONTROL

When gross and fine motor skills become more polished, children can participate and begin playing structured sports and exploring age-appropriate challenging movement activities with peers and on self. Movements that show coordination and balance in skipping, climbing, and running have children using their muscles in various and instrumental ways. This experience may be a good indicator that children who can experience this movement activity are on their way to progress forward and proficiently.

HEIGHT AND WEIGHT

In terms of height and weight, as children develop, height and weight variations are always examined in girls and boys. The thinking is that girls stopped growing at age 21 and boys stopped growing at age 25. Today, we are experiencing girls growing to about age 25 and growth spurt-topping out, while boys are stretching growth spurts to about age 27. Weight comes as growth and development begin topping out as the skeletal frame that we are born with, taking on the weight from our nutritional habits and our life fitness exercise regimen.

Muscle increase follows along with girl–boy scenario comparing height–weight variations. Muscle bulk shows more on girls when they are a pre-teen, and seeing the muscle amount on their trunks, arms, and legs, while for boys in pre-teens, notice a thinning out and minimal fat content. Girls will spread muscle mass early while developing, and when boys hit the same age of development, they spread muscle mass throughout their body in gaining height and less on weight gain.

© ESB Professional/Shutterstock.com

Physical activity is essential for the physical development of children, especially during their early growing years. Parents and educators need to begin to encourage children to participate in physical activities at an early age and build good habits that can last a lifetime. The following are some values:

- Benefits of physical activity for kids
- Physical and mental development
- Improvement of the overall health
- Child brain development
- Increased lung capacity
- Heart health

AN EFFECTIVE PHYSICAL PROGRAM FOR YOUNG CHILDREN

Young children need to have opportunities in being active and working to develop control, coordination, and movement. Specialists recommend children taking part in physical activities for about an hour every day to retain physical health.

We need to teach children at an early age to understand the importance of physical movement and activities that support mental and physical enhancement, including:

- Group activities
- Activity break
- Bone and muscle strengthening exercises
- Outdoor locations
- Movement and exploration
- Learning climate and environment playing activities

© wavebreakmedia/Shutterstock.com

WORKSHEET FOR CHAPTER 4

Research an article from a physical education journal on muscle growth and physical activity.

_____

_____

_____

_____

_____

_____

_____

_____

_____

_____

_____

_____

_____

_____

_____

_____

_____

_____

Chapter 5
QUALITY MOVEMENT AND PHYSICAL EDUCATION

© Robert Kneschke/Shutterstock.com

Quality physical education and physical activity programs are critical to the development and management of health fitness. The author believes that every child across of nation's education curriculum and programs, in preschool, to middle school, to high school into college, need to have access to participate in quality and effective physical education. The objective of physical education is to develop and achieve physically educated youth who attain knowledge, skills, confidence, self-esteem, self-image, and social-emotional to experience a lifetime of health, fitness, and developmental, physical activity. These principles outline the foundation to provide a positive learning climate and environment and quality program.

FOUR ESSENTIAL COMPONENTS OF QUALITY PHYSICAL EDUCATION

- Opportunity to learn – experiences, exploration, environment
- Meaningful content – comprehensible, age-appropriate, connectivity to motor skills
- Appropriate instruction – specificity, developmental pacing, curriculum-based movement
- Student and program Assessment – observation, task card objectives, process mastery

These benchmarks form the outline to observe and measure a starting point for learning movement, activities, and skills.

The five areas of fundamental body movement's exhibit are manipulative moves. These moves comprise of throwing, catching, kicking, passing, and dribbling. Children need to have physical education in their lives, as quality physical education programs are vital in increasing the physical competence, health, and fitness; self-accountability; and gratification of physical activity for all children to be physically active as lifetime fitness participants. Movement concepts come out of the curriculum delivering body awareness, spatial awareness, effort-and-response awareness, and a relationship of manipulatives and exploring peers and space. Movement learning strategies represent a range of methods that can assist a participant or team in attaining a movement competency successfully. When defining motor skills, we refer to walking, running, stretching, bending, catching, and throwing. They are the fundamental units of all movement activities in physical education classes, sports, and everyday life. The movement supports and builds an organization to develop strength, coordination, balance, motor thinking, and sensory systems. These abilities develop through change, becoming essential for supporting children management and attention in the both indoor and outdoor classrooms. Offering consistent physical education classes and activities to young children develops their movement development and skill performance for achieving competencies. In addition, benefits of regular physical activity assist children in improving cardiorespiratory fitness, strengthening bones and muscles, weight maintenance, lessen symptoms of anxiety and depression, and decrease the risk of developing health issues and illness prevention.

An essential purpose of health and fitness within a program for best practices is to teach and learn the knowledge and understanding, abilities, and attributes needed for mental, social-emotional, and physical competence for future involvement.

Indulgent aptitudes (soft skills) are a band of productive personality traits that characterize one's relationships in an environment where humans roam. These skills can include social graces, communication abilities, language skills, personal habits, cognitive or emotional empathy, emotional intelligence, time management, and teamwork and leadership traits. If these characteristics of an individual, co-worker, superior, parent, volunteer, and a student are not demonstrated in this environment, three things happen: meeting to bring this to the attention of the individual not exhibiting a genuine consideration for others, place them on improvement program, and, if behavior does not improve, dismiss them.

FUNDAMENTAL MOVEMENT SKILLS

- Balance skills – movements where the body remains in place but moves in horizontal and vertical axes
- Locomotor skills –running, jumping, hopping, skipping, and galloping
- Ball skills – catching, throwing, kicking, passing, striking, and dribbling
- Sports skills – sometimes known as "physical knowledge"; provides a child an opportunity to experience movement with poise and ability

TYPES OF MOVEMENT

- Abduction is a movement away from the center (spreading action of the toes or fingers apart).
- Adduction moves toward the middle of the body (bringing the fingers and toes together). (Adduction and abduction always refer to changes of the appendicular skeleton legs and limbs).
- Angular motion involves flexion, extension, adduction, and abduction. Each based on reference to a specific anatomical position.
- Flexion acts as bending or the condition of being bent, especially the bending of a limb or joint.
- Dorsiflexion and plantar flexion movements of the foot are the movement of the ankle (down) and plantar flexion movement of the ankle (pull back).
- Elevation–depression moving in a superior or inferior direction, as the mandible depressing (mouth open) and mandible elevated (mouth closed).
- Extension is same plane as flexion, except that it increases the angle between articulating elements. Expansion turns flexion.
- Hyperextension is a continuous action past the anatomical position, which can cause injury.
- Protraction moves part of the body anteriorly in the horizontal direction.
- Retracting turns movement of protraction pulling movement toward middle toward the center of the body.
- Rotation turns the body or a limb around the longitudinal axis, as rotating the arm to screw in a lightbulb.

UNDERSTANDING BIOMECHANICS

Biomechanics refers to studies of structure and function in seeking an understanding of mechanical aspects of biological schemes, at levels ranging from whole organisms to organs, cells, and cell organelles, consuming the methods of mechanics and relating to the movement and composition of living organisms. Biomechanics is a viewpoint into comprehending movement of bodies working within their networks of structural and functionality for production systems.

Sports biomechanics looks into analyzing professional athletes and sports engagement in general purpose. Biomechanics dissects structure and function of biological systems by way of techniques of mechanics involving physics related to forces and actions.

KEY PRINCIPLES OF BIOMECHANICS

- The principle of force
- The law of connected parts
- The principle of instinct causing motion
- The concept of stretch reduce cycle
- The principle of totaling joint forces

Biomechanics studies the science of movement of a living body, considering muscles, bones, tendons, and ligaments banding together to create change. Biomechanics aligns to kinesiology—the study of motion.

PRINCIPLES OF BIOMECHANIC INQUIRY

Stability focuses on the principle that the lower the center of mass, the larger the base of support, the center of mass to the bottom of support, and the higher the mass, the more stability surges. Maximum effort looks at the way movement is most often showing how to throw or move an object that may involve many parts of the area of the body. Maximum velocity produces of ultimate speed that uses body joints from the large to the small in the execution of this type of movement. Reaction connects time the capacity to respond rapidly to a motivator. Torque spends energy by more of a means of sufficient force for movement advantage.

Biomechanics studies movement of a living body, including how muscles, bones, tendons, and ligaments work together to move. This movement works to improve and advance the study of movement through measurable advancements.

Human movement studies how the human body operates, focusing on the effectiveness of body operation and activity movement for sport, fitness, and health. The inclusion of physiological, biomechanical, and psychological systems of the body contributes to the understanding of body movement and efficiency. The objective of biomechanics in sport and physical exercise is to develop performance efficiency in various sport or physical exercise.

COACHING MOTOR DEVELOPMENT

The value of forces brings a close connection between gravitational force and established force. The belief of equivalence is the basis for force, and it is a starting point for looking at power as included in biomechanics. Using and applying biomechanics to improve training techniques happens in two ways: Teachers, coaches, and trainers use experience and knowledge of mechanics for actions to be precise in students or athletes to execute a skill.

PRINCIPLE OF STABILITY

Stability patterns provide rules for athletes in skill positioning and for keeping balance fundamentals when running and jumping. Fundamentals outline and monitor training for improving developmental finesse of stances for both static and active balance.

BIOMECHANICS IN SPORT AND EXERCISE

Executing proper biomechanics for sport and exercise delivery in body movements and participant interaction needs experience and practice. Athletes need to be faster, quicker, jump higher. Biomechanics studies living body and its mechanics, also known as *kinesiology*—the study of movement relating to anatomy and physiology of exercise. In young children, we observe the focal points of attaining motor skills and incorporate teaching effectiveness and age-appropriate activities.

MAKING SENSE OF FORCE

The contribution of force is in causes of movement. When negative forces cause bad change, we analyze the effects that interrupted the foundation of that action. When athletes commit an error, this is cause to an incorrect application of force applied to that movement or action in performance or practice.

VALUES IN GENERAL, LINEAR, AND ANGULAR MOTION

Human movement forms or natural motion are fundamentally a blend of two effects: linear motion, movement from a straight line, and angular motion, movement from a circle (involves rotation). Angular motion, including dancing and ice and figure skating, consists of rotating around an axis. Linear is the starting point from which the movement and forces began to change. Looking at a steady line that transforms into a circle of pace and directional changes is learned. Practices and attainment in training activities start with the preparation of the move, execution of the action, and follow-through after the step.

© Iakov Filimonov/Shutterstock.com

Chapter 6
NUTRITION AND HYDRATION

© Photobac/Shutterstock.com

A meaningful look at nutrition for children is foundationally defining sound nutrients. They are elements that hold food to task for growing healthy, observing the developmental process, the effectiveness of fruits and vegetables and roles these elements play in keeping children growing and healthy for life-long health.

Listed below is a recommendation outline that pinpoints a plan of health:

Plan of Health	
Protein	Incorporate fish, trimmed and lean meats and chicken, eggs, beans, peas, and unsalted nuts and seeds.
Fruits	Add a mixture of fresh, canned, frozen or dried fruits, may be not so much juice as it contains sugar.
Vegetables	Integrate fresh, canned, frozen or dried vegetables of all sorts and colors.
Grains	Display and use barley for soups, brown rice, buckwheat flour mix, cracked wheat, millet, oatmeal, popcorn, and whole wheat breads and pasta.
Dairy	Use butter, cheese, cheese products, cultured dairy, yogurt, cottage cheese, sour cream, dips, cultured dairy foods, frozen desserts, ice cream, milk, nondairy beverages, whey, milk powder.

During childhood development, the importance of eyeing nutrition—fewer causes for children to exhibit less energy and less motivation for learning, which adversely effects intellectual development and academic achievement—needs to be a priority. In addition, inadequate nutrition affects physical growth and stage progress, regressing growth speed. The following nutrients support the body:

- Water
- Carbohydrates
- Protein and amino acids
- Fat
- Vitamins
- Minerals
- Omega-3 fatty acids
- Monitor iron levels

Young children need nutritious food to align growth and developmental requirements for a healthy beginning. Adults and practitioners recognize the importance of nutrition in balancing children's physical and mental development to grow strong. It starts with the parent in modeling this behavior for healthy eating.

Children today require a variety of whole foods, emphasizing sound minerals and vitamins, protein, and calcium. Weight in a child's development affects their progress of gaining or losing weight. Nutrition impacts cognitive ability and conduct in young children in school and while in movement activities. Nutrients make up a meal design supporting long-range effects and success depending on their focus and implementation.

There are two classes of nutrients: macronutrients and micronutrients. The three categories of macronutrients involve a makeup of carbohydrate, protein, and fat. The two types of micronutrients are vitamins and minerals, and these play a role in molecules that make cells create energy.

SEVEN SIGNS OF INSUFFICIENT NUTRITIONAL VALUE

- Unknown fatigue – Fatigue is a typical side effect; lack of iron deficiency can cause tiredness, leading to anemia, thus showing low levels of the red blood cells in the body
- Hair becomes dry and breakable
- Nail growth
- A problem of the mouth, teeth, and glands
- Soft to loose bowel movements
- Loss of appetite

Children need to safeguard practicing good nutritional habits as it is developmentally essential at all ages. Young children need to seek nutrients that support health and strength for growing and developing into able individuals physically and mentally through their life span. The dietary practices learned transfer into adulthood, so eating well and green will enhance a healthy and mental living environment reducing the chances of illness, disease, and weight issues.

NUTRITION AND LIVING

Today's families live by a schedule and often affect their meal plans or how families plan familial meals. Children's diets consist of accessibility and fast food, pickup, and ready-made packaged food. Not good food for the soul. This food contains unhealthy nutrients or lacks nutrients of value. Some issues in health care are caused by these types of foods and kind of eating habits that may turn into adulthood. Importance of eating healthy for young children and balancing physical and mental fitness is as follows:

- Balance energy
- Mental input
- Level of attitudes
- Support robust weight management
- Mental health preservation

MAKE MEAL TIMES A LIFE PRIORITY

We need to regain the concept of eating as a group sitting at the table, as a family unit, to create healthy eating habits, socialization, and relationship building. Eating times establish:

- Comfortable and safe environment
- Communication and sharing
- Evaluate food consumption
- Model conduct and behavior for your children

NUTRITION EDUCATION ACTIVITIES FOR CHILDREN

Children can be partners and may help with shopping for groceries and selecting foods with benefits. Model and teach children with reading food labels to introduce the world of eating healthy. Children need to connect to proper eating and take the role of owning their recognition of whole and green foods. Children like to play outdoors and experience nature. Young children love to play with dirt and water. Begin planting a vegetable garden that a child can nurture and maintain. They learn to care for the planting, work the soil, and add the amount of water needed to keep the garden hydrated. Trees that bear fruit can also be a project in securing space and locality to place a fruit tree nearby in the yard. By doing this, a partnership and ownership can be formed to support the nutritional importance of knowing how and where food comes from and how eating healthy keeps growing and fitness a real adventure.

The following is a focus outline that recommends how to engage children on the nutritional bandwagon exposing them to creating habits for nutritional values and health:

- Modeling nutritional behavior
- Introduce early
- Assess diet
- Knowing what to eat
- Eat and snack at plan times with limits
- Don't reward with food
- Limit TV and vid games
- Set snack boundaries

HYDRATION

© Maria Madrinan/Shutterstock.com

Hydration works to replenish water in the body to fuel all the measures of its human function. We do this by drinking water, sometimes chewing on ice bits, or consuming foods with high water content. We want to keep hydrated with fluids and water through each day and avoid dehydration by lacking the water amounts needed to perform adequately, and contributing to a well-oiled human machine. The human body contains 70% water. Water serves to regulate the body's temperature, breaking down food and expelling waste. The body loses water when you sweat, breathe, and urinate. It is essential to replace the water lost to avoid getting dehydrated. Young children dehydrate more easily than adults do. Lack of water can affect their stature, sweating, and dealing with heat. Children need to drink water regularly.

The following are some tips to use as a guide to hydration children:

1. Fluids dispersed in regular, small drinks
2. Eating soups, clear soda pop, or Gatorade
3. Water popsicles and ice bits
4. Continue a regular fluid regiment

Hydration is a crucial factor for children's health to proceed in their development and fitness. Water is a regulator for the human body, and our digestive system breaks down waste. It is essential to replenish the water and fluids you lose to prevent yourself from having low levels of water and liquids in your system. We need to keep an eye on children as they are at danger of reaching dehydration than older individuals and adults do.

The following is a heads-up of warning signs for dehydration in children:

- Heavy colored urine
- Lack of urine for eight hours
- Dry skin, lips, and mouth
- Eyes inflammation
- Fatigue and lack of energy
- Listlessness
- Pasty dry cotton moisture
- Headaches
- Lack of attention span
- Constipation

The amount of water your child requires depends on different aspects of a child's developmental stature, age, and level of activity and fitness. Children aged 8 years need 4–6 or 6–8 glasses of water to keep them hydrated; however, children are active in organized sports activities, so they will need to have more fluids and hydrated both before and after a sporting event.

Drinking water is the best practice in keeping children hydrated during their day at school, home, and at play. Water is a thirst quencher, whereas other liquids like milk, juice, and flavored beverages can help to hydrate children, keep hydrated as a rule of thumb every day. The fluids young children drink, and the whole green foods that children eat, with proper rest, maintain a healthy functioning system that supports the development of the heart, brain, muscles, and skeletal growth.

If children have an issue with drinking water, there are a variety of drinking fluids children can get into and stay hydrated, including:

1. Water, of course
2. Electrolyte-infused fluids
3. Children's electrolyte – Pedialyte
4. All favored Gatorade
5. Watermelon
6. Coconut water
7. Veggie-based water content samples

Fruit juices contain sugar and may distress the stomach unless diluted with water. Sports drinks can be beneficial, but you need to read what they include. Children can reach for these types of beverages because they taste good. Sport participation requires liquid requirements of less than 60 total minutes needing water, more than 60 full minutes, a well-contained beneficial sports drink containing electrolytes and carbohydrates for energy and hydration. Benefits of maintaining hydration helps children be at their fitness level during competition and training. It helps children regulate their body temperature against heat contact and sickness.

© Sergey Novikov/Shutterstock.com

Chapter 7

THE LEARNING ENVIRONMENT

The learning environment is crucial for children's learning and their adaptation to school success. A safe, open, and fostering climate is a necessary supportive measure of learning and development for young children. These environments help to assist build behaviors and child conduct in serving as a central part of involvements for all children, including children with disabilities. In early childhood education programs, preschool children connect with learning environments where they development interactions with teachers who take care of them and keep them safe, in order to learn and be creative in their developmental experiences. A constructive and connectivity in children's environmental setting provides opportunities to observe preschool-age children's needs while they play at instructional centers in the classroom, where a science table, dramatic play, block area, and water work activities support the mental movement about learning. The significance of the environment delivers a synopsis of what to form to create and sustain developmentally appropriate preschool learning environmental settings. Being heads-up in sizing up the learning environments for young children allows the learners to explore and tap into their background. Connect aspects of their setting that are comfortable and safe for learning and expression, and always support the learning environment in the age-appropriate process of activity development.

Coaching, working, and developing motor skills advance young children's ability to learn and explore their learning setting. The learning environment influences children's dealings and has an impact on their behavior. Develop a learning setting where children can play freely and use their imaginary expression to add social-emotional positive feelings to the learning environment. A productive and quality learning environment consists of children exposed to the social interaction among their peers, teachers, staff, and the program. The program also includes the physical and its makeup and structure, professional and consistent instructional staff, leadership that needs to be proactive, advocates, and managerial. The program should address the age-appropriate curriculum and support parenting and the family makeup. A teacher is a foundational asset in building the learning environment and setting the climate for young children to experience and develop their learning. In the learning environment, essential elements such as having children asking questions support the questioning and simple connectable answers. Share various ways that ideas and student expression demonstrate objectivity and observation. The delivery of teaching needs to have multiple entries and exits, meaning it strives to go further than the classroom. Discovering using both indoor classroom and outdoor classroom sets a balance of learning for young children where they can integrate both environments.

The outdoor classroom supports experience, exploration, and imagination, giving children opportunities to problem solve, create, and take risks on trying different things. Learning should be more participatory and applicable to young children. We as supporters of young children want to see them develop into responsible and contributing citizens to society.

The outdoor classroom brings together playing and learning supporting children to learn about and gain respect for nature. The outdoor environment for preservation of human beings, animals that live in their habitat, and resident plants serves as connectors to young children's education. Space is a magic word for the outdoor environment and helps children to appreciate the outdoor climate and learning. Outdoor space and play offer children exploration of the outdoors, nature, and the area where they embody self-esteem, muscle strength, balance, and coordination.

Some tips for incorporating the outdoor classroom into a young child's learning capacity are children work to achieve better marks in school, their fitness and development improve constantly, stress and anxiety levels decrease, and children show enthusiasm and motivation to play, have fun, and learn to develop skills in movement. The child's self- image begins to form in their attitudes, and behavior tends to work with self-regulation for environmental acquisition. Language begins to develop with the help of terminology and describing objects, communication skills developing among peers practice talking to one another. The outdoor environment is the experiential opportunity for young children to learn in an open-air class that will benefit their fitness, health, and respect for nature.

© Rawpixel.com/Shutterstock.com

COMPETING

When is it time for children to understand competition? How do children prepare to compete in games, play, and organized activities?

The "L" word "losing" needs to be taught in a supportive and comprehensive manner to children that losing is OK. Begin by praising efforts and laying out the activities to be fun. This should be done at an early age as children are experiencing and developing their awareness radar. Build concepts of scenarios that involve the maybe's and what-if's as a teaching moment to enable children to see, feel, and think about not always coming out ahead. Children need to be exposed to role modeling in the area of fair play, honesty, and sportsmanship. Many times, in dealing with feelings, anger frustration may result. Self-regulation can lead to management skills in the emotional aspect of anger and also arrogance. The growing need to feel the win at an early age not only propels them to explore good feelings about themselves but also understands that children cannot win all the time. Help in not letting them win all the time, do not make a temper tantrum and issue, be a humble winner, and keep this practice of winning versus losing until maturing can take over.

In this area of competition, take on behavior whether good or bad. Keep a check on responses and attitudes, looking for good sportsmanship and fair play. Teach able opportunities always need to be available. Teach children, players, and teams to support one another, those with much potential and skill especially. Introduce tolerance to those who are acutely able in skill performance, be adaptable to those who are less competent but are learning.

Teaching that losing games can be supportive of children serves to deal with empathy and compassion. When children win, they get better at sports activities and learn something new that advances their emotional development.

Losing teams can be a challenge to children when they are not shown support and taught to understand a team concept value. The team concept value represents the bonding and role fulfilling participation that a group takes on collectively for a challenge. Individual and joint feelings show be valued, and blame needs to be absent from a loss. Talking to friends and family can add light from their perspective on how the event went. Staying loyal to your team and the team concept value will build strength and comradery.

Losing in our life span is a part of life, teaching us to lose gracefully means not always comes simple. Winning places athletes in a position to attempt to improve and gain success at competing levels. Losing evaluates how to make a change and obtain an evaluation. This is part of the world that children experience in the area of competition.

COMPETITION CAN BE GOOD AND BAD FOR CHILDREN

Game challenges the personal worth when you lose. When you win, you feel as though you are on top of the world, but a win is only as good as your last win. A loss stays with you and banks experience as to how not to do it again. Self-worth works to keep the persona moving steady and forward. Completion can challenge stability and consistency when it comes to feeling good about oneself. Winning and losing are temporary experiences and may not support the well-being of the individual. Therefore, the thinking is too much on presentation and very little on the process and human development.

We all take a careful look at the competition to see what it is teaching to benefit our children in society. Winning is a unique, yet limited result. Only one team or individual can achieve victory for the day. When unproductive children place emotions of self-esteem in competition, losing can be low. Their self-image is second-hand looked upon as not competent. The fear is the will to put effort into attempts in competition. How competing is taught will be an indicator of how the child will move forward in the game.

Competition is accepted and looked at in society as normal behavior. Competition has been around for hundreds and hundreds of years. It is a human way of measuring one another like most animals do when battling for territory. The most straight forward approach to comprehend this competitive attitude is to see how children will be successful by doing excellent work or by defeating others in rivalry events to secure the win.

All children like to be good at something, whether it be favorite in the family, best at academics, sports, music, art, or most beautiful or fashionable. Good coaches instruct children to good sportsmanship, classroom teachers and parents rarely address competition issues in the home or classroom. Children struggling to cope with the competition are more likely to be scolded for jealous feelings, instead of receiving assistance in how to deal with healthy jealousy. Calling children "jealous"

may cause them to lose hope and confidence, thus stealing from them their abilities to initiate healthy involvement in competitive activities. They may feel like losers and feel guilty for wishing they could win.

COMPETITION IN THE FAMILY, LIFE, AND SCHOOL

We need to stress cooperation, instead of competition. Young children should be cheered to be supportive of family members, and parents can work on this collectively. They can view their sibling's achievements as something in which they can share. Teaching brothers and sisters to support for family performances is an exemplary method in meeting up with children's challenging emotions of sibling competitiveness.

Children can come from and live in highly stressful and competitive family's units achieving many events of victories, but a perspective on winning needs to have a focus. And achieve in many activities, but winning needs view. It's good for children to use brilliance and work on it, but need not feel prized only for their achievement.

Parents need to be suitable models and select participation activities that don't always pursue winning. Respect your opponents, not with fear, but with consideration for the skills they may have. Every parent can tell their children they can accomplish anything they want to do, but need to put the time and effort in executing success. The ability to function in a competition is midpoint to school and lifelong attainment. Parents need to teach their children to be tough. Children can pick up creative outlooks of failures and losses as learning experiences and skill recognition. Balance competitive participatory events with noncompetitive experiences for learning and enjoyment.

Let parents help their children to deal with losses by looking at their competitive mode and interest. We want to get away from blaming teachers and coaches of children's challenges for expecting them to handle their responsibilities.

Children need to be taught to explore alternatives for their losses or failures in activities they choose. Every child has areas in which they are successful and skillfully useful. Children shouldn't embody insecurity or fear setbacks and should not get too much sympathy. Talking about children's losses may need to wait until after the feeling and tensions have dissipated to escape angry responses. Parents need to give time to children's learning in this stage of their development.

Tips for approaching children in the upside of the win–loss performance thinking:

Use a questioning method, instead of a lecture delivery, this helps children comprehend that (1) one cannot always win, (2) disappointment does not equal failures, (3) the current experience was not fruitful, (4) not all have the savvy, and (5) the main idea and feeling is to play the learning game at your best to land competitive significance.

In closing and adding to the challenge of understanding competition and the subareas of winning and losing, it is paramount that children are given opportunities with peers and individually to experience and explore the rebounding affects that winning brings to success and understand the correctness to this mental and physical development in children.

© Lorelyn Medina/Shutterstock.com

SUMMARY OF MOTOR LEARNING DEVELOPMENT, FITNESS, AND DEVELOPMENT

The thinking in motor learning is when multiplex progressions in the brain communicate to recall an experience of a recorded skill making changes in the nervous system that lets room for action of a motor skill.

Examples of motor learning, skills, and behaviors are without thought involuntarily recollected retentions. When we go for a walk, great example. Walking is a vast involved motor action and multifaceted movement that we take for granted but executed it to the fullest of motor ability. Adding to what we know, motor control transmits nerve drive out of the motor cortex to motor components, which coordinates merging of muscles, while motor learning work to improve motor skills, the practice suave and consistent movements.

The importance and foundational workings of motor learning goals take into consideration the environmental and undertaking challenges play in influencing movement. This support provides a practicing level for developing learning for purpose and objectives that drive improving motor skills and development in children.

4

7

3

8

7

X

1

3

2

4